50 Italian Noodle Dishes

By: Kelly Johnson

Table of Contents

- Spaghetti Aglio e Olio
- Fettuccine Alfredo
- Lasagna
- Pappardelle with Bolognese Sauce
- Linguine with Clams
- Tagliatelle al Ragù
- Penne alla Vodka
- Ravioli di Ricotta e Spinaci
- Cavatelli with Sausage and Broccoli Rabe
- Tortellini in Brodo
- Gnocchi al Pesto
- Fettuccine Bolognese
- Spaghetti Carbonara
- Pappardelle with Wild Boar Ragù
- Bucatini all'Amatriciana
- Orecchiette with Broccoli Rabe and Sausage
- Lasagna alla Bolognese
- Fagottini with Lemon and Ricotta
- Farfalle with Creamy Tomato Sauce
- Cannelloni with Spinach and Ricotta
- Pasta alla Norma
- Capellini Pomodoro
- Spaghetti with Meatballs
- Tagliatelle al Tartufo (Truffle)
- Penne arrabbiata
- Pappardelle with Mushroom Sauce
- Ravioli with Brown Butter and Sage
- Trofie al Pesto
- Maltagliati with Beans and Sausage
- Spaghetti alle Vongole
- Agnolotti with Butter and Parmesan
- Pici all'Aglione
- Fettuccine ai Funghi
- Spaghetti Puttanesca
- Fusilli with Sausage and Mushrooms
- Cavatelli with Ricotta

- Lasagna di Verdure (Vegetable Lasagna)
- Ramen alla Romana
- Fagottini with Mushrooms and Truffle
- Bucatini with Guanciale
- Cannelloni with Meat Filling
- Tagliatelle with Lobster
- Orecchiette with Tomato and Basil
- Ravioli with Squash and Sage
- Spaghetti alla Chitarra
- Fusilli with Pesto Genovese
- Gnocchi with Gorgonzola Sauce
- Pappardelle with Duck Ragù
- Fettuccine alla Panna
- Torta di Noodles (Noodle Pie)

Spaghetti Aglio e Olio

Ingredients:

- 1 lb spaghetti
- 1/4 cup extra virgin olive oil
- 4 garlic cloves, thinly sliced
- 1/2 teaspoon red pepper flakes
- Salt, to taste
- Fresh parsley, chopped
- Freshly grated Parmesan cheese (optional)

Instructions:

1. Cook the spaghetti according to the package instructions. Reserve 1 cup of pasta cooking water and drain the rest.
2. In a large skillet, heat olive oil over medium heat. Add garlic and cook until golden and fragrant, about 2 minutes.
3. Add red pepper flakes and cook for another 30 seconds.
4. Add the cooked spaghetti to the skillet, along with the reserved pasta water. Toss to combine.
5. Season with salt and garnish with fresh parsley. Serve with grated Parmesan cheese, if desired.

Fettuccine Alfredo

Ingredients:

- 1 lb fettuccine
- 1 cup heavy cream
- 1/2 cup unsalted butter
- 1 cup freshly grated Parmesan cheese
- Salt and freshly ground black pepper, to taste
- Fresh parsley, chopped (for garnish)

Instructions:

1. Cook the fettuccine according to the package instructions. Drain, reserving 1/2 cup of pasta cooking water.
2. In a large skillet, melt butter over medium heat. Add the cream and bring it to a simmer.
3. Reduce the heat and cook for 5-6 minutes, allowing the sauce to thicken.
4. Stir in Parmesan cheese until smooth. Add pasta water to adjust the sauce's consistency, if needed.
5. Add the fettuccine and toss to coat. Season with salt and pepper to taste.
6. Garnish with fresh parsley and serve.

Lasagna

Ingredients:

- 12 lasagna noodles, cooked
- 1 lb ground beef or pork
- 1 onion, chopped
- 2 cloves garlic, minced
- 2 cups marinara sauce
- 15 oz ricotta cheese
- 1 egg
- 3 cups shredded mozzarella cheese
- 1/2 cup grated Parmesan cheese
- 1/4 cup fresh basil, chopped
- Salt and pepper, to taste

Instructions:

1. Preheat the oven to 375°F (190°C).
2. In a large skillet, brown the ground meat with the onion and garlic. Drain any excess fat.
3. Add marinara sauce to the meat mixture and simmer for 10 minutes. Season with salt and pepper.
4. In a bowl, combine ricotta cheese, egg, mozzarella, Parmesan, and basil. Mix until smooth.
5. In a baking dish, layer marinara sauce, lasagna noodles, ricotta mixture, and mozzarella cheese. Repeat the layers, finishing with a layer of sauce and mozzarella on top.
6. Cover with foil and bake for 25 minutes. Remove foil and bake for another 25 minutes, until bubbly and golden.
7. Let it cool for 10 minutes before serving.

Pappardelle with Bolognese Sauce

Ingredients:

- 1 lb pappardelle
- 2 tbsp olive oil
- 1 onion, chopped
- 2 carrots, chopped
- 2 celery stalks, chopped
- 3 cloves garlic, minced
- 1 lb ground beef and pork mixture
- 1 cup red wine
- 2 cups crushed tomatoes
- 1/2 cup whole milk or heavy cream
- Salt and pepper, to taste
- Fresh basil, chopped (for garnish)

Instructions:

1. Cook pappardelle according to package instructions.
2. In a large skillet, heat olive oil over medium heat. Add onion, carrots, celery, and garlic. Cook until softened, about 5 minutes.
3. Add the ground meat and cook until browned. Pour in red wine and cook for 5 minutes.
4. Stir in crushed tomatoes, bring to a simmer, and cook for 30 minutes. Add milk or cream to make the sauce richer.
5. Season with salt and pepper. Serve the sauce over pappardelle and garnish with fresh basil.

Linguine with Clams

Ingredients:

- 1 lb linguine
- 2 tbsp olive oil
- 4 cloves garlic, minced
- 1/4 cup dry white wine
- 1 lb fresh clams, scrubbed
- 1/2 tsp red pepper flakes (optional)
- Fresh parsley, chopped
- Salt and pepper, to taste

Instructions:

1. Cook linguine according to package instructions.
2. In a large pan, heat olive oil over medium heat. Add garlic and cook for 1-2 minutes until fragrant.
3. Pour in the wine and bring to a simmer. Add clams and cover. Cook for 5-7 minutes, until the clams open.
4. Add cooked linguine to the pan and toss. Season with salt, pepper, and red pepper flakes.
5. Garnish with fresh parsley and serve immediately.

Tagliatelle al Ragù

Ingredients:

- 1 lb tagliatelle
- 2 tbsp olive oil
- 1 onion, chopped
- 1 carrot, chopped
- 2 cloves garlic, minced
- 1 lb ground beef or pork
- 1/2 cup red wine
- 2 cups tomato sauce
- 1/2 cup milk or cream
- Salt and pepper, to taste
- Fresh basil, for garnish

Instructions:

1. Cook tagliatelle according to package instructions.
2. In a large skillet, heat olive oil over medium heat. Add onion, carrot, and garlic, cooking until soft.
3. Add ground meat and cook until browned. Pour in wine and cook until it reduces by half.
4. Add tomato sauce and simmer for 20 minutes. Stir in milk or cream to finish the sauce.
5. Season with salt and pepper. Toss the ragù with the tagliatelle and garnish with basil.

Penne alla Vodka

Ingredients:

- 1 lb penne pasta
- 2 tbsp olive oil
- 1 onion, chopped
- 2 cloves garlic, minced
- 1/2 cup vodka
- 1 can (14 oz) crushed tomatoes
- 1/2 cup heavy cream
- Salt and pepper, to taste
- Fresh parsley, chopped

Instructions:

1. Cook the penne pasta according to package instructions.
2. In a large skillet, heat olive oil over medium heat. Add onion and garlic, cooking until soft.
3. Pour in vodka and cook for 2 minutes, allowing the alcohol to evaporate.
4. Stir in crushed tomatoes and simmer for 10 minutes. Add heavy cream and cook for another 5 minutes.
5. Season with salt and pepper. Toss the penne with the sauce and garnish with fresh parsley.

Ravioli di Ricotta e Spinaci

Ingredients:

- 1 package fresh or frozen ravioli (ricotta and spinach filling)
- 2 tbsp olive oil
- 2 cloves garlic, minced
- 1/2 cup vegetable broth or chicken broth
- 1/2 cup heavy cream
- Salt and pepper, to taste
- Fresh Parmesan cheese, for garnish

Instructions:

1. Cook ravioli according to package instructions.
2. In a large skillet, heat olive oil over medium heat. Add garlic and cook until fragrant.
3. Pour in the broth and bring to a simmer. Stir in heavy cream and cook until the sauce thickens slightly.
4. Season with salt and pepper. Toss the cooked ravioli in the sauce and serve with grated Parmesan.

Cavatelli with Sausage and Broccoli Rabe

Ingredients:

- 1 lb cavatelli
- 1 tbsp olive oil
- 2 sausages, casings removed
- 2 cloves garlic, minced
- 1 bunch broccoli rabe, trimmed and chopped
- Salt and pepper, to taste
- Fresh Parmesan cheese, for garnish

Instructions:

1. Cook cavatelli according to package instructions.
2. In a large skillet, heat olive oil over medium heat. Add sausage and cook until browned, breaking it apart as it cooks.
3. Add garlic and broccoli rabe. Cook until the broccoli is tender, about 5 minutes.
4. Season with salt and pepper. Toss the cavatelli with the sausage and broccoli rabe mixture.
5. Garnish with fresh Parmesan and serve.

Tortellini in Brodo

Ingredients:

- 1 lb tortellini (fresh or frozen)
- 4 cups chicken broth or vegetable broth
- 1/2 cup grated Parmesan cheese
- Salt and pepper, to taste
- Fresh parsley, chopped

Instructions:

1. Bring the broth to a simmer in a large pot.
2. Add the tortellini to the broth and cook according to package instructions.
3. Season with salt and pepper to taste.
4. Serve hot, topped with Parmesan cheese and fresh parsley.

Gnocchi al Pesto

Ingredients:

- 1 lb potato gnocchi (store-bought or homemade)
- 1/4 cup olive oil
- 2 cups fresh basil leaves
- 2 cloves garlic
- 1/4 cup pine nuts
- 1/2 cup freshly grated Parmesan cheese
- Salt and pepper, to taste

Instructions:

1. Cook gnocchi according to package instructions, then drain and set aside.
2. In a food processor, combine basil, garlic, pine nuts, Parmesan, salt, and pepper. Blend while slowly adding olive oil until smooth.
3. Toss the cooked gnocchi in the pesto sauce until well coated. Serve immediately.

Fettuccine Bolognese

Ingredients:

- 1 lb fettuccine
- 2 tbsp olive oil
- 1 onion, chopped
- 2 carrots, chopped
- 2 celery stalks, chopped
- 2 cloves garlic, minced
- 1 lb ground beef and pork mixture
- 1/2 cup red wine
- 2 cups tomato sauce
- 1/2 cup milk or cream
- Salt and pepper, to taste
- Fresh basil or parsley, chopped for garnish

Instructions:

1. Cook the fettuccine according to package instructions.
2. In a large skillet, heat olive oil over medium heat. Add onion, carrots, celery, and garlic, cooking until softened.
3. Add the ground meat and cook until browned. Pour in wine and cook for 5 minutes to reduce.
4. Stir in tomato sauce and simmer for 20 minutes. Add milk or cream and cook for another 5 minutes.
5. Season with salt and pepper. Toss the fettuccine with the sauce and garnish with fresh herbs.

Spaghetti Carbonara

Ingredients:

- 1 lb spaghetti
- 4 oz pancetta or guanciale, chopped
- 3 large eggs
- 1 cup grated Parmesan or Pecorino Romano cheese
- Salt and pepper, to taste
- Fresh parsley, chopped (for garnish)

Instructions:

1. Cook spaghetti according to package instructions, reserving some pasta water.
2. In a skillet, cook pancetta or guanciale over medium heat until crispy, then set aside.
3. In a bowl, whisk together eggs, cheese, salt, and pepper.
4. Toss the cooked spaghetti with the pancetta and a little pasta water, then pour in the egg mixture. Toss quickly to create a creamy sauce.
5. Serve with extra cheese and fresh parsley.

Pappardelle with Wild Boar Ragù

Ingredients:

- 1 lb pappardelle
- 2 tbsp olive oil
- 1 lb wild boar, chopped into small pieces
- 1 onion, chopped
- 2 carrots, chopped
- 2 celery stalks, chopped
- 3 cloves garlic, minced
- 1 cup red wine
- 2 cups tomato sauce
- 1/2 cup heavy cream
- Salt and pepper, to taste
- Fresh parsley, chopped (for garnish)

Instructions:

1. Cook the pappardelle according to package instructions.
2. In a large pot, heat olive oil over medium heat. Add wild boar and brown it on all sides.
3. Add onion, carrots, celery, and garlic, cooking until softened.
4. Pour in wine and cook for 5 minutes. Add tomato sauce and simmer for 1 hour, or until the meat is tender.
5. Stir in cream and season with salt and pepper.
6. Toss the pappardelle with the ragù and garnish with fresh parsley.

Bucatini all'Amatriciana

Ingredients:

- 1 lb bucatini pasta
- 2 tbsp olive oil
- 1 onion, chopped
- 4 oz guanciale or pancetta, chopped
- 1 can (14 oz) crushed tomatoes
- 1/2 cup dry white wine
- 1/2 tsp red pepper flakes (optional)
- Salt and pepper, to taste
- Fresh Pecorino Romano cheese, grated for garnish

Instructions:

1. Cook the bucatini according to package instructions.
2. In a skillet, heat olive oil over medium heat. Add onion and cook until softened.
3. Add guanciale and cook until crispy. Pour in wine and cook until it reduces.
4. Stir in crushed tomatoes and red pepper flakes. Simmer for 20 minutes.
5. Toss the bucatini with the sauce and season with salt and pepper.
6. Serve with grated Pecorino Romano cheese.

Orecchiette with Broccoli Rabe and Sausage

Ingredients:

- 1 lb orecchiette pasta
- 2 tbsp olive oil
- 1 lb Italian sausage (bulk or casings removed)
- 4 cloves garlic, minced
- 1 bunch broccoli rabe, chopped
- 1/4 tsp red pepper flakes (optional)
- Salt and pepper, to taste
- Fresh Parmesan cheese, grated for garnish

Instructions:

1. Cook the orecchiette according to package instructions.
2. In a skillet, heat olive oil over medium heat. Add sausage and cook until browned.
3. Add garlic and red pepper flakes, cooking until fragrant.
4. Add broccoli rabe and cook until wilted.
5. Toss the orecchiette with the sausage and broccoli rabe mixture. Season with salt and pepper.
6. Garnish with Parmesan cheese before serving.

Lasagna alla Bolognese

Ingredients:

- 12 lasagna noodles, cooked
- 2 cups Bolognese sauce (recipe above)
- 1 lb ricotta cheese
- 2 cups mozzarella cheese, shredded
- 1/2 cup grated Parmesan cheese
- Salt and pepper, to taste

Instructions:

1. Preheat oven to 375°F (190°C).
2. In a baking dish, layer Bolognese sauce, lasagna noodles, ricotta cheese, mozzarella, and Parmesan. Repeat layers.
3. Finish with a top layer of sauce and cheese.
4. Cover with foil and bake for 25 minutes. Remove foil and bake for another 25 minutes.
5. Let cool for 10 minutes before slicing.

Fagottini with Lemon and Ricotta

Ingredients:

- 1 package fresh fagottini pasta (or any square-shaped pasta)
- 1 cup ricotta cheese
- Zest of 1 lemon
- 2 tbsp fresh basil, chopped
- Salt and pepper, to taste
- 1/4 cup olive oil
- 2 cloves garlic, minced
- Fresh Parmesan cheese, grated for garnish

Instructions:

1. Cook the fagottini according to package instructions.
2. In a bowl, mix ricotta, lemon zest, basil, salt, and pepper.
3. In a pan, heat olive oil and sauté garlic until fragrant.
4. Toss the cooked fagottini in the garlic oil, then stir in the ricotta mixture.
5. Serve with freshly grated Parmesan cheese.

Farfalle with Creamy Tomato Sauce

Ingredients:

- 1 lb farfalle pasta
- 2 tbsp olive oil
- 1 onion, chopped
- 2 cloves garlic, minced
- 1 can (14 oz) crushed tomatoes
- 1/2 cup heavy cream
- Salt and pepper, to taste
- Fresh basil, chopped (for garnish)

Instructions:

1. Cook farfalle according to package instructions.
2. In a skillet, heat olive oil over medium heat. Add onion and garlic, cooking until softened.
3. Stir in crushed tomatoes and cook for 10 minutes.
4. Add heavy cream, salt, and pepper. Simmer for another 5 minutes.
5. Toss the farfalle with the sauce and garnish with fresh basil.

Cannelloni with Spinach and Ricotta

Ingredients:

- 12 cannelloni tubes
- 2 cups ricotta cheese
- 2 cups cooked spinach, chopped
- 1/2 cup grated Parmesan cheese
- 2 cups marinara sauce
- 1/2 cup mozzarella cheese, shredded
- Salt and pepper, to taste

Instructions:

1. Preheat oven to 375°F (190°C).
2. Cook the cannelloni tubes according to package instructions.
3. In a bowl, mix ricotta, spinach, Parmesan, salt, and pepper.
4. Stuff the cannelloni with the ricotta mixture and place in a baking dish.
5. Pour marinara sauce over the cannelloni, sprinkle with mozzarella, and bake for 25 minutes.
6. Let cool for 5 minutes before serving.

Pasta alla Norma

Ingredients:

- 1 lb pasta (rigatoni or penne)
- 2 eggplants, diced
- 1/4 cup olive oil
- 3 cloves garlic, minced
- 1 can (14 oz) crushed tomatoes
- Salt and pepper, to taste
- Fresh basil, chopped (for garnish)
- Ricotta salata, grated (for garnish)

Instructions:

1. Cook the pasta according to package instructions.
2. In a skillet, heat olive oil over medium heat. Add eggplant and cook until soft and golden.
3. Add garlic and crushed tomatoes, cooking for 10 minutes. Season with salt and pepper.
4. Toss the pasta with the sauce and eggplant mixture.
5. Garnish with fresh basil and grated ricotta salata.

Capellini Pomodoro

Ingredients:

- 1 lb capellini (angel hair) pasta
- 2 tbsp olive oil
- 3 cloves garlic, minced
- 4 cups ripe tomatoes, chopped (or 1 can of crushed tomatoes)
- 1/4 cup fresh basil, chopped
- Salt and pepper, to taste
- Grated Parmesan cheese (optional)

Instructions:

1. Cook the capellini according to package instructions.
2. In a large pan, heat olive oil over medium heat. Add garlic and cook for 1 minute until fragrant.
3. Add chopped tomatoes and cook for 5-7 minutes until the sauce thickens.
4. Toss the cooked pasta into the tomato sauce, mixing in fresh basil.
5. Season with salt and pepper, and serve with grated Parmesan cheese.

Spaghetti with Meatballs

Ingredients:

- 1 lb spaghetti
- 1 lb ground beef
- 1/2 cup breadcrumbs
- 1 egg
- 2 cloves garlic, minced
- 1/4 cup grated Parmesan cheese
- 1 jar marinara sauce
- Fresh basil, chopped (for garnish)
- Salt and pepper, to taste

Instructions:

1. Preheat the oven to 375°F (190°C). Mix ground beef, breadcrumbs, egg, garlic, Parmesan, salt, and pepper in a bowl. Shape into meatballs.
2. Place the meatballs on a baking sheet and bake for 15-20 minutes, until cooked through.
3. While the meatballs are baking, cook the spaghetti according to package instructions.
4. Heat marinara sauce in a large pan. Add the meatballs and simmer for 10 minutes.
5. Toss the cooked spaghetti in the sauce and serve with fresh basil.

Tagliatelle al Tartufo (Truffle)

Ingredients:

- 1 lb tagliatelle pasta
- 2 tbsp butter
- 2 tbsp olive oil
- 1/2 cup heavy cream
- 1/4 cup grated Parmesan cheese
- 1/4 cup truffle oil (or shaved fresh truffle)
- Salt and pepper, to taste

Instructions:

1. Cook the tagliatelle according to package instructions.
2. In a large pan, melt butter and olive oil over medium heat.
3. Add heavy cream and simmer for 5 minutes. Stir in grated Parmesan cheese and truffle oil (or shaved truffle).
4. Toss the cooked tagliatelle in the creamy truffle sauce.
5. Season with salt and pepper to taste and serve.

Penne Arrabbiata

Ingredients:

- 1 lb penne pasta
- 2 tbsp olive oil
- 4 cloves garlic, minced
- 1 tsp red pepper flakes
- 1 can (14 oz) crushed tomatoes
- Salt and pepper, to taste
- Fresh parsley, chopped for garnish

Instructions:

1. Cook the penne according to package instructions.
2. In a pan, heat olive oil over medium heat. Add garlic and red pepper flakes, cooking for 1 minute.
3. Add the crushed tomatoes and simmer for 10-15 minutes.
4. Toss the cooked penne in the arrabbiata sauce and mix well.
5. Season with salt and pepper, and garnish with fresh parsley.

Pappardelle with Mushroom Sauce

Ingredients:

- 1 lb pappardelle pasta
- 2 tbsp olive oil
- 1 lb mixed mushrooms (such as cremini, shiitake, or button), sliced
- 2 cloves garlic, minced
- 1/2 cup dry white wine
- 1/2 cup heavy cream
- Fresh thyme, chopped
- Salt and pepper, to taste
- Grated Parmesan cheese (optional)

Instructions:

1. Cook the pappardelle according to package instructions.
2. In a pan, heat olive oil over medium heat. Add mushrooms and cook until tender, about 5-7 minutes.
3. Add garlic and cook for another minute. Stir in white wine and simmer until reduced by half.
4. Add heavy cream and fresh thyme, and simmer for 5 minutes until the sauce thickens.
5. Toss the cooked pappardelle into the mushroom sauce. Season with salt and pepper and serve with grated Parmesan cheese.

Ravioli with Brown Butter and Sage

Ingredients:

- 1 lb ravioli (store-bought or homemade)
- 1/2 cup unsalted butter
- 10 fresh sage leaves
- 1/4 cup grated Parmesan cheese
- Salt and pepper, to taste

Instructions:

1. Cook the ravioli according to package instructions.
2. In a pan, melt the butter over medium heat until it turns golden brown and starts to smell nutty (about 3-5 minutes).
3. Add the sage leaves and cook for 1 minute until crispy.
4. Toss the cooked ravioli into the brown butter and sage sauce. Season with salt and pepper.
5. Serve with grated Parmesan cheese.

Trofie al Pesto

Ingredients:

- 1 lb trofie pasta
- 2 cups fresh basil leaves
- 1/4 cup pine nuts
- 1/2 cup grated Parmesan cheese
- 1/4 cup olive oil
- 2 cloves garlic
- Salt and pepper, to taste

Instructions:

1. Cook the trofie according to package instructions.
2. In a blender or food processor, combine basil, pine nuts, Parmesan cheese, garlic, and olive oil. Blend until smooth. Season with salt and pepper.
3. Toss the cooked trofie in the pesto sauce and serve with extra Parmesan cheese.

Maltagliati with Beans and Sausage

Ingredients:

- 1 lb maltagliati pasta
- 2 tbsp olive oil
- 1 lb Italian sausage, crumbled
- 1 can (15 oz) cannellini beans, drained and rinsed
- 2 cups chicken broth
- 1/4 cup fresh parsley, chopped
- Salt and pepper, to taste

Instructions:

1. Cook the maltagliati according to package instructions.
2. In a pan, heat olive oil over medium heat. Add crumbled sausage and cook until browned.
3. Stir in the beans and chicken broth, simmering for 10 minutes.
4. Toss the cooked pasta into the sausage and bean mixture.
5. Season with salt and pepper, and garnish with fresh parsley.

Spaghetti alle Vongole

Ingredients:

- 1 lb spaghetti
- 2 tbsp olive oil
- 2 cloves garlic, minced
- 1 lb fresh clams, scrubbed
- 1/2 cup dry white wine
- 1/4 cup fresh parsley, chopped
- Lemon zest, for garnish
- Salt and pepper, to taste

Instructions:

1. Cook the spaghetti according to package instructions.
2. In a pan, heat olive oil over medium heat. Add garlic and cook until fragrant.
3. Add clams and white wine, cover, and cook until clams open (about 5 minutes).
4. Toss the cooked spaghetti in the clam sauce. Garnish with parsley and lemon zest.

Agnolotti with Butter and Parmesan

Ingredients:

- 1 lb agnolotti pasta (typically filled with meat or cheese)
- 1/2 cup unsalted butter
- 1/4 cup grated Parmesan cheese
- Fresh thyme or sage, for garnish
- Salt and pepper, to taste

Instructions:

1. Cook the agnolotti according to package instructions.
2. In a pan, melt butter over medium heat until it starts to bubble and brown.
3. Toss the cooked agnolotti in the browned butter and mix well.
4. Season with salt and pepper, and garnish with fresh thyme or sage and grated Parmesan cheese.

Pici all'Aglione

Ingredients:

- 1 lb pici pasta (or any thick, hand-rolled pasta)
- 4 tbsp olive oil
- 6 cloves garlic, sliced
- 1 can (14 oz) crushed tomatoes
- 1 tsp red pepper flakes
- Salt and pepper, to taste
- Fresh parsley, chopped for garnish
- Grated Pecorino Romano cheese (optional)

Instructions:

1. Cook the pici pasta according to package instructions.
2. In a large pan, heat olive oil over medium heat. Add garlic and cook until fragrant.
3. Add crushed tomatoes and red pepper flakes. Simmer for 15-20 minutes, stirring occasionally.
4. Season with salt and pepper. Toss the cooked pasta into the sauce and mix well.
5. Garnish with fresh parsley and Pecorino Romano if desired.

Fettuccine ai Funghi

Ingredients:

- 1 lb fettuccine pasta
- 2 tbsp olive oil
- 1 lb mixed mushrooms, sliced
- 2 cloves garlic, minced
- 1/2 cup heavy cream
- 1/2 cup vegetable or chicken broth
- 1/4 cup grated Parmesan cheese
- Fresh parsley, chopped
- Salt and pepper, to taste

Instructions:

1. Cook the fettuccine according to package instructions.
2. In a large pan, heat olive oil over medium heat. Add mushrooms and cook until soft and browned.
3. Add garlic and cook for 1 minute. Stir in the cream and broth, simmering for 10 minutes.
4. Toss the pasta into the mushroom sauce, adding Parmesan cheese.
5. Season with salt, pepper, and garnish with fresh parsley.

Spaghetti Puttanesca

Ingredients:

- 1 lb spaghetti
- 2 tbsp olive oil
- 4 cloves garlic, minced
- 1/2 tsp red pepper flakes
- 1 can (14 oz) crushed tomatoes
- 1/4 cup Kalamata olives, pitted and sliced
- 2 tbsp capers
- 4 anchovy fillets, minced (optional)
- Salt and pepper, to taste
- Fresh parsley, chopped for garnish

Instructions:

1. Cook the spaghetti according to package instructions.
2. In a pan, heat olive oil over medium heat. Add garlic and red pepper flakes, cooking for 1 minute.
3. Add crushed tomatoes, olives, capers, and anchovies. Simmer for 15 minutes.
4. Toss the cooked pasta into the sauce and mix well.
5. Season with salt and pepper, garnish with fresh parsley.

Fusilli with Sausage and Mushrooms

Ingredients:

- 1 lb fusilli pasta
- 2 tbsp olive oil
- 1 lb Italian sausage, casing removed
- 1/2 lb mushrooms, sliced
- 2 cloves garlic, minced
- 1/2 cup white wine
- 1/2 cup heavy cream
- Salt and pepper, to taste
- Fresh thyme, chopped for garnish
- Grated Parmesan cheese for serving

Instructions:

1. Cook the fusilli pasta according to package instructions.
2. In a pan, heat olive oil over medium heat. Add sausage and cook until browned.
3. Add garlic and mushrooms, cooking until mushrooms are softened.
4. Pour in white wine, simmer for 5 minutes, then add cream and cook for 10 more minutes.
5. Toss the cooked pasta into the sauce, season with salt and pepper, and garnish with fresh thyme and Parmesan cheese.

Cavatelli with Ricotta

Ingredients:

- 1 lb cavatelli pasta
- 1 cup ricotta cheese
- 1/4 cup grated Parmesan cheese
- 2 tbsp olive oil
- 1/4 tsp nutmeg
- Fresh basil, chopped for garnish
- Salt and pepper, to taste

Instructions:

1. Cook the cavatelli pasta according to package instructions.
2. In a large bowl, mix ricotta cheese, Parmesan cheese, olive oil, nutmeg, salt, and pepper.
3. Toss the cooked pasta into the ricotta mixture until well coated.
4. Garnish with fresh basil.

Lasagna di Verdure (Vegetable Lasagna)

Ingredients:

- 1 lb lasagna noodles
- 2 tbsp olive oil
- 1 onion, diced
- 2 cloves garlic, minced
- 1 zucchini, sliced
- 1 eggplant, diced
- 2 cups spinach
- 1/2 cup ricotta cheese
- 2 cups marinara sauce
- 1 1/2 cups mozzarella cheese, shredded
- 1/4 cup Parmesan cheese, grated
- Salt and pepper, to taste

Instructions:

1. Preheat the oven to 375°F (190°C).
2. Cook the lasagna noodles according to package instructions.
3. In a pan, heat olive oil over medium heat. Add onion and garlic, cooking until softened.
4. Add zucchini, eggplant, and spinach, cooking until tender. Season with salt and pepper.
5. In a baking dish, layer the noodles, vegetable mixture, ricotta, marinara sauce, and mozzarella. Repeat the layers.
6. Top with Parmesan cheese and bake for 25-30 minutes, until the cheese is golden and bubbly.

Ramen alla Romana

Ingredients:

- 1 lb ramen noodles
- 4 cups chicken broth
- 2 tbsp soy sauce
- 1 tbsp miso paste
- 1/4 cup heavy cream
- 2 eggs
- 1/4 cup grated Parmesan cheese
- Fresh basil, chopped for garnish
- Salt and pepper, to taste

Instructions:

1. Cook the ramen noodles according to package instructions.
2. In a pot, heat the chicken broth over medium heat. Add soy sauce and miso paste, stirring to dissolve.
3. Stir in heavy cream and bring to a simmer. Add salt and pepper to taste.
4. Cook the eggs in boiling water for 6 minutes to make soft-boiled eggs.
5. Assemble the ramen by adding noodles to the broth, topping with soft-boiled eggs, Parmesan, and fresh basil.

Fagottini with Mushrooms and Truffle

Ingredients:

- 1 lb fagottini (or other filled pasta)
- 2 tbsp butter
- 1 lb mushrooms, sliced
- 1/4 cup truffle oil
- 1/4 cup grated Parmesan cheese
- Salt and pepper, to taste

Instructions:

1. Cook the fagottini according to package instructions.
2. In a pan, melt butter over medium heat and sauté the mushrooms until soft.
3. Drizzle in the truffle oil and toss to coat.
4. Add the cooked pasta to the mushrooms and toss to combine.
5. Season with salt and pepper, and garnish with Parmesan.

Bucatini with Guanciale

Ingredients:

- 1 lb bucatini pasta
- 1/2 lb guanciale, sliced into small pieces
- 2 cloves garlic, minced
- 1/2 cup white wine
- 1/4 tsp red pepper flakes
- 1/2 cup grated Pecorino Romano cheese
- Salt and pepper, to taste

Instructions:

1. Cook the bucatini according to package instructions.
2. In a pan, heat olive oil and sauté the guanciale until crispy.
3. Add garlic and red pepper flakes, cooking for 1 minute.
4. Pour in the white wine and simmer for 5 minutes.
5. Toss the cooked pasta into the sauce and mix well. Season with salt and pepper.
6. Garnish with Pecorino Romano cheese.

Cannelloni with Meat Filling

Ingredients:

- 12 cannelloni tubes
- 1 lb ground beef
- 1/2 onion, diced
- 2 cloves garlic, minced
- 1/2 cup ricotta cheese
- 1/4 cup grated Parmesan cheese
- 2 cups marinara sauce
- Salt and pepper, to taste

Instructions:

1. Preheat the oven to 375°F (190°C).
2. Cook the cannelloni tubes according to package instructions.
3. In a pan, sauté onion and garlic in olive oil. Add ground beef and cook until browned.
4. Stir in ricotta and Parmesan cheese. Season with salt and pepper.
5. Stuff the cannelloni with the meat mixture and place them in a baking dish.
6. Pour marinara sauce over the stuffed cannelloni and bake for 25-30 minutes.

Tagliatelle with Lobster

Ingredients:

- 1 lb tagliatelle pasta
- 2 lobster tails, cooked and chopped
- 2 tbsp olive oil
- 2 cloves garlic, minced
- 1/2 cup white wine
- 1/2 cup heavy cream
- Zest of 1 lemon
- Fresh parsley, chopped for garnish
- Salt and pepper, to taste
- Grated Parmesan cheese (optional)

Instructions:

1. Cook the tagliatelle according to package instructions.
2. In a large pan, heat olive oil over medium heat. Add garlic and cook until fragrant.
3. Add white wine and simmer for 2-3 minutes.
4. Stir in the heavy cream and simmer for 5 minutes. Season with salt and pepper.
5. Add the chopped lobster and toss to combine.
6. Drain the pasta and toss with the lobster sauce. Garnish with lemon zest, fresh parsley, and Parmesan cheese.

Orecchiette with Tomato and Basil

Ingredients:

- 1 lb orecchiette pasta
- 2 tbsp olive oil
- 3 cloves garlic, minced
- 2 cups cherry tomatoes, halved
- 1/2 cup fresh basil, chopped
- 1/4 cup grated Parmesan cheese
- Salt and pepper, to taste

Instructions:

1. Cook the orecchiette according to package instructions.
2. In a pan, heat olive oil over medium heat. Add garlic and cook for 1 minute.
3. Add the cherry tomatoes and cook until soft, about 5 minutes.
4. Toss the pasta into the sauce, mixing in the fresh basil.
5. Season with salt and pepper and garnish with grated Parmesan cheese.

Ravioli with Squash and Sage

Ingredients:

- 1 lb ravioli (butternut squash or pumpkin filling)
- 2 tbsp butter
- 10 fresh sage leaves
- 1/4 cup grated Parmesan cheese
- Salt and pepper, to taste

Instructions:

1. Cook the ravioli according to package instructions.
2. In a large pan, melt the butter over medium heat. Add the sage leaves and cook until crispy.
3. Toss the cooked ravioli into the sage butter and mix gently.
4. Season with salt and pepper and garnish with grated Parmesan cheese.

Spaghetti alla Chitarra

Ingredients:

- 1 lb spaghetti alla chitarra (or any square spaghetti)
- 2 tbsp olive oil
- 2 cloves garlic, minced
- 1/2 tsp red pepper flakes
- 1 can (14 oz) crushed tomatoes
- Fresh basil, chopped for garnish
- Salt and pepper, to taste

Instructions:

1. Cook the spaghetti alla chitarra according to package instructions.
2. In a pan, heat olive oil over medium heat. Add garlic and red pepper flakes, cooking for 1 minute.
3. Add crushed tomatoes and simmer for 15-20 minutes.
4. Toss the cooked pasta into the sauce and mix well.
5. Season with salt and pepper, garnish with fresh basil.

Fusilli with Pesto Genovese

Ingredients:

- 1 lb fusilli pasta
- 2 cups fresh basil leaves
- 1/4 cup pine nuts
- 1/2 cup grated Parmesan cheese
- 1/4 cup olive oil
- 2 cloves garlic
- Salt and pepper, to taste

Instructions:

1. Cook the fusilli according to package instructions.
2. In a blender or food processor, combine basil, pine nuts, Parmesan cheese, garlic, and olive oil. Blend until smooth. Season with salt and pepper.
3. Toss the cooked pasta with the pesto sauce. Serve with additional Parmesan cheese.

Gnocchi with Gorgonzola Sauce

Ingredients:

- 1 lb gnocchi
- 1/2 cup Gorgonzola cheese, crumbled
- 1/4 cup heavy cream
- 2 tbsp butter
- 1/4 cup chopped walnuts (optional)
- Salt and pepper, to taste

Instructions:

1. Cook the gnocchi according to package instructions.
2. In a pan, melt the butter over medium heat. Add Gorgonzola cheese and heavy cream, stirring until smooth.
3. Toss the cooked gnocchi into the sauce and mix gently.
4. Season with salt and pepper and garnish with chopped walnuts.

Pappardelle with Duck Ragù

Ingredients:

- 1 lb pappardelle pasta
- 2 tbsp olive oil
- 1 lb duck breast, cooked and shredded
- 1 onion, diced
- 2 cloves garlic, minced
- 1 cup red wine
- 1 can (14 oz) crushed tomatoes
- 1/4 cup fresh rosemary, chopped
- Salt and pepper, to taste

Instructions:

1. Cook the pappardelle according to package instructions.
2. In a large pan, heat olive oil over medium heat. Add onion and garlic, cooking until softened.
3. Add the shredded duck and cook for 5 minutes.
4. Pour in red wine and simmer for 5 minutes. Stir in crushed tomatoes and rosemary, and simmer for 15 minutes.
5. Toss the cooked pasta into the ragù and mix well. Season with salt and pepper.

Fettuccine alla Panna

Ingredients:

- 1 lb fettuccine pasta
- 2 tbsp butter
- 1/2 cup heavy cream
- 1/2 cup grated Parmesan cheese
- Salt and pepper, to taste

Instructions:

1. Cook the fettuccine according to package instructions.
2. In a pan, melt the butter over medium heat. Add heavy cream and bring to a simmer.
3. Stir in the grated Parmesan cheese until smooth and creamy.
4. Toss the cooked pasta into the sauce and mix well.
5. Season with salt and pepper.

Torta di Noodles (Noodle Pie)

Ingredients:

- 1 lb egg noodles
- 2 tbsp butter
- 1 onion, diced
- 1/2 lb ground beef or pork
- 1/2 cup ricotta cheese
- 1/2 cup grated Parmesan cheese
- 1 egg, beaten
- 1/4 cup milk
- Salt and pepper, to taste

Instructions:

1. Preheat the oven to 375°F (190°C).
2. Cook the egg noodles according to package instructions.
3. In a pan, melt butter over medium heat. Add onion and cook until softened.
4. Add ground meat and cook until browned. Season with salt and pepper.
5. In a bowl, mix ricotta, Parmesan, egg, and milk. Stir in the cooked noodles and meat mixture.
6. Pour into a greased pie dish and bake for 25-30 minutes, until golden and set.

www.ingramcontent.com/pod-product-compliance
Lightning Source LLC
LaVergne TN
LVHW081340060526
838201LV00055B/2754